LEARN ABOUT VALUES

HONESTY

by Cynthia Roberts

Published in the United States of America by The Child's World®
1980 Lookout Drive • Mankato, MN 56003-1705 • 800-599-READ • www.childsworld.com

The Child's World®: Mary Berendes, Publishing Director; Katherine Stevenson, Editor
The Design Lab: Kathy Petelinsek, Art Director; Julia Goozen, Design and Page Production

Photo Credits: © Michael Keller/Corbis: cover
All other photos: © David M. Budd Photography

Library of Congress Cataloging-in-Publication Data
Roberts, Cynthia, 1960–
  Honesty / by Cynthia Roberts.
    p. cm. — (Learn about values)
  ISBN 978-1-59296-671-4 ISBN 1-59296-671-3 (library bound: alk. paper)
  I. Honesty—Juvenile literature. 2. Values—Juvenile literature. I. Title. II. Series.
  BJ1533.H7R63 2006
  179'.9—dc22   2006000958

CONTENTS

What Is Honesty?

Have you ever told a lie? Have you ever tried to cheat? Everyone has times when they could lie or cheat. But honesty means telling the truth. It means not cheating. Honesty is not always easy. It takes strength. But it is the right thing to do. And it feels good!

4

Honesty feels better than cheating!

Honesty at School

Your teacher gives you homework. She tells you to do it over the weekend. You end up playing with friends. You forget all about your homework! On Monday, your teacher asks for the homework. You show honesty by telling the truth. You do not make **excuses**. You do not **copy** another student's work.

Sometimes telling the truth can be scary.

Money Mistakes

Maybe you like to go to the store after school. Your **favorite** gum costs 50 cents. You give the clerk one dollar. She should give you 50 cents back. But she gives you 75 cents by mistake. You know she gave you too much money. You show honesty by telling her she made a mistake. You give the extra money back.

Honesty means not taking more than your share.

Honesty **and Cheating**

You are playing a board game. You are unhappy because your friend is winning. He goes to the kitchen for a snack. You could move your piece farther ahead. Then you might win! But you show honesty by not cheating. You follow the rules—even if it means you will lose. Maybe you will win next time!

Knowing you have played honestly feels better than cheating.

Honesty and Waiting

The swirly slide is the best thing on the playground. Kids are lined up, waiting to use it. You are waiting your turn. The person in front of you looks the other way. There is room in front of her. She might not notice it you went ahead. You show honesty by waiting your turn.

Honesty means being fair about taking your turn.

13

Taking the Cake

Your dad has baked chocolate cake. He made it to take to a party. Chocolate cake is your favorite! It looks really good, and you are hungry. You eat a piece. Your mom sees that some is missing. She wants to know who ate it. You could blame your baby brother. But you show honesty by telling the truth.

Honesty means telling the truth—even if you will get in trouble!

15

Honesty at Home

Your older brother has some money. He leaves it on the table by mistake. It would be easy to take it. You could put it in your piggy bank. He would not know where the money went. But you show honesty by leaving the money alone. You tell your brother where he left it.

Honesty means not taking things that belong to others.

Honesty and the Lost-and-Found

You and your friends are playing at the park. You see a bag near the swings. There are toys in the bag! Somebody has left them by mistake. You would love to have some of the toys. But you know they belong to someone else. You show honesty by taking them to the lost-and-found.

18

Honesty means returning things that are not yours.

19

Honesty Is Important!

Honesty shows people that you tell the truth. It shows others that they can trust you. People want friends who are honest. They want family members who are honest, too. People will trust you when they know you tell the truth!

It is nice to be trusted!

glossary

copy
When you copy something, you do it exactly as it is done somewhere else.

excuses
Excuses are reasons why you did not do something.

favorite
When you like something best, it is your favorite.

books

Leany, Cindy. *Lost and Found: A Story about Honesty* (Hero Club series). Vero Beach, FL: Rourke, 2003.

Nettleton, Pamela Hill. *Is That True? Kids Talk about Honesty* (Kids Talk series). Minneapolis, MN: Picture Window Books, 2004.

Park, Barbara. *Junie B., First Grader: Cheater Pants.* New York: Random House, 2003.

web sites

Visit our Web page for links about character education and values:
http://www.childsworld.com/links

Note to parents, teachers, and librarians:
We routinely check our Web links to make sure they're safe, active sites—so encourage your readers to check them out!

index

about the author

Even as a child, Cynthia Roberts knew she wanted to be a writer. She is always working to involve kids in reading and writing, and she loves spending time in the children's section of the library or bookstore. Cynthia enjoys gardening, traveling, and having fun with friends and family.

D1537484